Yahoo! Through the Ages

The Rise, Fall, and Reinvention of an Internet Giant

Authored by

Zahid Ameer

Published by

Goodword eBooks

DEDICATION

"I dedicate this book to my beloved parents, whose wisdom
I hold in the highest regard. Their every word of guidance
has been a beacon of light, illuminating the path of my life
and shaping the essence of who I am."

Yahoo! Through the Ages

Contents:

Introduction

In the mid-1990s, the internet was a frontier in its infancy. The World Wide Web, as it was then called, was an uncharted and largely experimental space, filled with raw potential but also with uncertainty. Access to the internet was limited, web pages were sparse and basic, and users often had difficulty navigating the growing number of websites. In this environment, few companies truly understood how to harness the power of the internet and shape it into something that could be used easily by everyday people. One company that did was Yahoo!.

Yahoo! was founded in January 1994 by Jerry Yang and David Filo, two electrical engineering graduate students at Stanford University. What began as a personal project to categorize and organize interesting websites quickly transformed into something much larger. Their creation, originally called "Jerry and David's Guide to the World Wide Web," was intended to help users find useful and relevant websites in an era when there was no clear way to navigate the web. The internet was like a vast, sprawling library with no catalog or order, and Yahoo! sought to fix that by acting as an organized directory that categorized websites into easily searchable categories.

In April 1994, Yang and Filo renamed their creation "Yahoo!" The name itself was derived from a backronym for "Yet Another Hierarchical Officious Oracle," but the term "yahoo" also resonated with the founders for its playful and irreverent connotation, symbolizing a fun and user-friendly approach to navigating the web. Yahoo! quickly gained traction among internet users because it filled a critical need for order in the web's chaotic expansion. Within months, the directory's popularity soared, and Yahoo! became the go-to resource for web navigation, attracting the attention of investors.

In March 1995, Yahoo! was incorporated as a company and soon secured its first round of venture capital funding from Sequoia Capital. From that point on, Yahoo!'s rise seemed unstoppable. By 1996, Yahoo! went public, with its Initial Public Offering (IPO) marking one of the defining moments of the dot-com era. This move not only brought in millions of dollars in investment capital but also cemented Yahoo!'s place as one of the internet's pioneering giants.

The company's early success wasn't just about providing a directory—it was about understanding the potential of the web and expanding Yahoo! into a broader platform. Yahoo! grew beyond a simple search directory to include services like Yahoo! Mail, Yahoo! News, Yahoo! Finance, and Yahoo! Sports. Each of these services became immensely popular and helped solidify Yahoo!'s reputation as the most important portal on the internet. By the late 1990s, Yahoo! had become a household name and was synonymous with the internet experience. It wasn't just a search engine; it was an entry point to the web itself.

During its peak, Yahoo! seemed to epitomize the boundless optimism and innovation of the dot-com boom. With millions of users flocking to its services daily, Yahoo! was at the center of a digital revolution that promised to change how people lived, worked, and communicated. The company grew rapidly, expanding its workforce and diversifying its offerings. Yahoo! made strategic acquisitions, forged partnerships, and expanded its global presence. By the late 1990s, it was one of the most visited websites in the world, and its stock price surged, making it one of the most valuable companies of the dot-com era.

But as the tech world evolved, Yahoo! faced a series of challenges. The dot-com bubble, which had inflated the value of many internet companies to unsustainable levels, burst in 2000, sending shockwaves through the tech industry. Yahoo!, like many other companies, saw its stock price plummet, but it managed to survive the crash. However, it was soon faced with a much more formidable challenge: the rise of Google. Google's innovative approach to search technology revolutionized how people found information online, and Yahoo!'s early dominance in web search began to erode.

Despite these challenges, Yahoo! continued to innovate and expand into new areas, launching services like Yahoo! Messenger and Yahoo! Groups, while also maintaining its core focus on content and email. Yet, the company struggled to keep pace with its more nimble competitors. Missed opportunities, such as its failure to acquire Google or Facebook in their early days, left Yahoo! trailing behind as new giants of the internet emerged.

As the 2000s progressed, Yahoo! went through a period of leadership changes, strategic pivots, and attempts to reclaim its dominance. One of the most notable efforts came in 2012 when Yahoo! appointed Marissa Mayer, a former Google executive, as CEO. Mayer embarked on an ambitious plan to revitalize the company, focusing on mobile services and high-profile acquisitions, such as the purchase of the blogging platform Tumblr. While some of these efforts showed promise, they were not enough to reverse Yahoo!'s decline.

In 2016, Yahoo! was sold to Verizon for $4.8 billion, marking the end of its era as an independent company. Verizon merged Yahoo! with AOL, creating a new media division called Oath, later renamed Verizon Media. Despite this, many of Yahoo!'s core services, such as Yahoo! Finance, Yahoo! Sports, and Yahoo! Mail, continued to thrive, serving millions of users worldwide.

This book chronicles the full arc of Yahoo!'s journey—from its meteoric rise in the early days of the internet, to its fall from dominance, to its ongoing efforts to reinvent itself in an ever-changing digital landscape. Yahoo!'s story is one of innovation, opportunity, and resilience. It is a tale of how a company, once at the top of the tech world, faced monumental challenges but refused to fade away. It is also a story that offers valuable lessons about the nature of the tech industry, the importance of adaptability, and the role that timing, vision, and leadership play in the success or failure of a company.

In the chapters that follow, we will explore the key moments in Yahoo!'s history—the decisions, the innovations, the triumphs, and the setbacks—that shaped the company and the broader internet landscape. From its early days as a humble web directory to its transformation into a global media and tech giant, Yahoo! has left an indelible mark on the internet's evolution. Through this detailed exploration, we aim to offer readers an in-depth understanding of Yahoo!'s impact, not just as a company, but as a cultural and technological force that helped shape the digital age.

As we look back at Yahoo!'s story, we see not only the rise and fall of a once-mighty internet empire but also the ongoing reinvention of a company that refuses to be forgotten. Yahoo! may no longer be the dominant player it

Yahoo! Through the Ages
once was, but its legacy endures, and its future remains a
fascinating chapter in the ever-evolving story of the
internet.

Chapter 1: The Dawn of Yahoo! – How It All Began

In the mid-1990s, the internet was still a relatively new frontier, an uncharted digital world filled with both promise and confusion. At the time, finding useful information on the web was like trying to navigate through a dense forest without a map. This was the challenge that two Stanford University graduate students, Jerry Yang and David Filo, set out to solve. What began as a hobby project to organize their favorite websites quickly transformed into a groundbreaking creation that would revolutionize the way people interacted with the internet.

The Birth of Yahoo!

The origins of Yahoo! date back to January 1994, when Yang and Filo developed a simple web directory as a way to manage their personal collection of favorite websites. They initially called it "Jerry and David's Guide to the World Wide Web," an unassuming name that reflected the simplicity of their project. Their guide was essentially a manually compiled list of links to websites that they found useful or interesting, categorized into topics and subtopics. The internet was a much smaller place then, with only a few thousand websites, but it was growing rapidly, and so was the number of users searching for content.

The directory started as a personal tool for Yang and Filo, but they quickly realized its broader potential. Early internet users, faced with the chaotic growth of websites, were in desperate need of a better way to navigate the web. The existing search engines were primitive, and there was no consistent method for organizing content. As more people began using their guide, the demand for a user-friendly way to explore the web became apparent. What started as a side project quickly gained popularity.

The Name "Yahoo!"

By March 1995, "Jerry and David's Guide" had evolved beyond a personal tool—it was becoming a public resource, a gateway to the World Wide Web. With its growing popularity, Yang and Filo knew they needed a more memorable and marketable name. They settled on "Yahoo!", an acronym for "Yet Another Hierarchical Officious Oracle." The term "Yahoo!" also reflected the fun and somewhat irreverent attitude they wanted their brand to embody. The word itself, derived from Jonathan Swift's *Gulliver's Travels*, described crude or unsophisticated beings, but to Yang and Filo, it conveyed excitement and spontaneity.

The exclamation point in "Yahoo!" added an element of dynamism and energy to the brand, setting it apart from more formal, business-like names. The company's quirky name was an immediate hit, capturing the spirit of the early web: playful, creative, and bursting with potential.

The Internet in 1994: A New Frontier

To understand the significance of Yahoo!'s creation, it's essential to appreciate the state of the internet in 1994. The web was in its infancy, with only around 3,000 websites in existence. Most users were academics or tech enthusiasts who had the technical know-how to navigate this new digital world. The average person, however, found the internet intimidating and difficult to use. Search engines like WebCrawler and Lycos were starting to emerge, but they were still rudimentary by modern standards, offering only keyword-based searches with limited accuracy.

In this environment, Yahoo!'s directory stood out as a revolutionary tool. Unlike search engines, which relied on algorithms to find web pages based on keywords, Yahoo! organized websites into categories and subcategories, making it easy for users to browse through topics of interest. Whether someone was looking for news, sports, entertainment, or business resources, Yahoo! offered a curated selection of websites in each category, saving users the frustration of sifting through irrelevant or low-quality content.

Yahoo!'s focus on human curation—rather than automated algorithms—set it apart from the competition. Each website in the directory was carefully reviewed and categorized by real people, which gave the platform a sense of reliability and quality. Users trusted Yahoo! to guide them to the best resources on the web, and this trust quickly turned Yahoo! into one of the most popular destinations on the internet.

Yahoo! Goes Public: Incorporation and Venture Capital

As Yahoo! grew in popularity, Yang and Filo realized that their project had outgrown its original scope. What had started as a hobby was now attracting millions of users, and the duo saw the potential to turn their creation into a thriving business. In March 1995, Yahoo! officially incorporated as a company. To fuel its rapid growth, the newly-formed Yahoo! needed funding, and they found a key partner in venture capital firm Sequoia Capital, known for its investments in other technology pioneers like Apple, Oracle, and Cisco.

Sequoia's investment of nearly $2 million in Yahoo! provided the company with the resources it needed to expand. This infusion of capital allowed Yahoo! to hire a professional management team, enhance its technology, and scale its operations to meet the growing demand. With Sequoia's backing, Yahoo! set its sights on becoming the definitive portal for the internet.

Yahoo! also brought on Tim Koogle as CEO, an experienced Silicon Valley executive who had worked at Motorola. Koogle's arrival was crucial in transforming Yahoo! from a small start-up into a full-fledged business. Under his leadership, Yahoo! developed a clear business strategy and began focusing on expanding its range of services to include news, email, finance, and more.

A Gateway to the Web: Yahoo!'s Explosive Growth

The period between 1995 and 1997 marked a time of explosive growth for Yahoo!. The company expanded its directory to include a wider array of categories, covering everything from news and sports to shopping and entertainment. As the internet continued to grow at an unprecedented rate, so did Yahoo!'s user base. By 1996, Yahoo! was handling millions of visitors a day, becoming a central hub for anyone looking to explore the web.

One of the key factors behind Yahoo!'s rapid rise was its user-friendly interface. At a time when many websites were cluttered and difficult to navigate, Yahoo! offered a clean, intuitive layout that made it easy for users to find what they were looking for. The homepage featured a simple search bar, along with a directory of categories that allowed users to browse through topics. This combination of search functionality and human-curated navigation made Yahoo! the go-to portal for millions of internet users.

In April 1996, Yahoo! went public with an initial public offering (IPO) on the NASDAQ, raising $33.8 million and giving the company a market capitalization of $848 million. The IPO was a watershed moment, not only for Yahoo! but for the entire tech industry. It signaled the dawn of the dot-com era, a time when internet companies were seen as the future of business and innovation.

The Importance of Yahoo! Mail

One of Yahoo!'s most significant innovations during its early years was the introduction of Yahoo! Mail in 1997. At the time, email was becoming an essential part of internet communication, and Yahoo! Mail quickly became one of the most popular free email services on the web. Offering unlimited storage and easy-to-use features, Yahoo! Mail attracted millions of users and became a core component of Yahoo!'s suite of services.

Yahoo! Mail not only brought more users to the platform but also helped increase engagement. Once users signed up for an email account, they were more likely to use other Yahoo! services, such as news, sports, and finance. This cross-pollination of services helped Yahoo! become a central part of users' online experience.

Conclusion: From Humble Beginnings to Internet Titan

Yahoo!'s early success was built on the vision of Jerry Yang and David Filo, who saw the potential of the internet long before most people even knew what it was. By creating a simple yet powerful directory of websites, they helped make the internet accessible to millions of users. Their focus on user experience, combined with strategic business decisions and a little bit of luck, allowed Yahoo! to become one of the first internet giants.

The company's incorporation in 1995 and its IPO in 1996 set the stage for what would become one of the most successful and influential companies of the early internet age. But as the internet landscape continued to evolve, Yahoo! would face new challenges that would test its ability to adapt and survive in an increasingly competitive market. This chapter marks the beginning of Yahoo!'s journey from a simple web directory to a global tech giant. The next chapters will explore the meteoric rise that followed and the challenges that lay ahead.

Chapter 2: Yahoo! Takes the Internet by Storm

In the late 1990s, the internet was undergoing a period of rapid expansion, and Yahoo! emerged as a dominant player, riding the wave of technological innovation and growing consumer interest. With its user-friendly interface, innovative services, and wide range of products, Yahoo! became synonymous with the internet for millions of people. From its launch as a simple web directory to its diversification into news, finance, sports, and entertainment, Yahoo! captured the imagination of early internet users and transformed how people interacted with the web.

Yahoo!'s Web Directory: The Gateway to the Internet

At the core of Yahoo!'s early success was its web directory, which categorized websites into a hierarchical structure, making it easier for users to find information in an increasingly vast and disorganized internet. In the mid-1990s, most people had little knowledge of how to navigate the web, and Yahoo! provided an accessible entry point. Rather than relying on search algorithms, Yahoo!'s directory was organized manually by a team of editors, ensuring that only relevant and high-quality sites were listed.

This curation made Yahoo! unique and highly trusted. Users could find websites on topics ranging from technology to entertainment with just a few clicks, and as the internet grew, so did Yahoo!'s directory. By the late 1990s, Yahoo! had expanded its directory to cover millions of sites, becoming a comprehensive hub of information for users across the globe.

Yahoo! Mail: Revolutionizing Online Communication

In 1997, Yahoo! made a strategic move that would transform its business and cement its place as an internet giant: the launch of Yahoo! Mail. At a time when email services were often paid or tied to specific internet service providers, Yahoo! Mail offered users something revolutionary—free, web-based email. This service allowed people to access their inboxes from any computer, as long as they had an internet connection. It was a game-changer in the way people communicated online.

Yahoo! Mail was an instant success, rapidly gaining millions of users and becoming one of the most popular email services in the world. Its appeal was bolstered by generous storage limits, user-friendly design, and integration with other Yahoo! services. Yahoo!'s early dominance in the email space gave it a significant advantage, helping it to build a massive user base that would later translate into opportunities for advertising revenue and product integration.

By the end of the 1990s, Yahoo! Mail had become a primary communication tool for millions of people, creating a loyal customer base that relied on Yahoo! not just as a search directory, but as a comprehensive internet service provider.

Expansion of Yahoo!'s Product Offerings

Yahoo! didn't stop at email. Recognizing the potential of the internet to serve as a platform for a wide variety of services, Yahoo! embarked on an aggressive expansion of its product offerings in the late 1990s. The company understood that to become the go-to portal for internet users, it needed to offer more than just search and email. It needed to provide content and services that would keep users coming back day after day.

Yahoo! News, launched in 1996, quickly became a popular source of online information, aggregating stories from multiple news outlets and offering users a diverse range of perspectives. With Yahoo! Finance, the company tapped into the growing interest in financial markets during the tech boom, providing real-time stock quotes, news, and analysis. Yahoo! Sports became a major hub for sports fans, offering news, scores, and fantasy sports leagues.

Yahoo! Games provided a platform for users to play online games, further broadening its appeal.

Each of these products brought in new users and increased the time people spent on Yahoo!. The company's strategy of diversifying its offerings created a virtuous cycle—users who came for one service were often exposed to others, increasing their engagement with Yahoo! as a whole.

The Portal Phenomenon: Yahoo! Becomes the Internet's Hub

By the late 1990s, Yahoo! had successfully positioned itself as the ultimate web portal—a one-stop-shop for everything users needed online. Whether they wanted to check the news, send an email, look up stock quotes, or play a game, Yahoo! offered it all in one place. This comprehensive approach differentiated Yahoo! from other internet companies, many of which focused on niche services or specific markets.

Yahoo!'s portal model was incredibly effective in the early days of the internet. The company understood that as people became more familiar with the web, they would seek out services that streamlined their experience. Instead of visiting multiple sites for different needs, users flocked to Yahoo! because it consolidated everything under one roof. Yahoo! became the default homepage for millions of users, and the company's user base skyrocketed as a result.

Yahoo!'s Initial Public Offering (IPO): A Defining Moment

Yahoo!'s rapid growth and success culminated in its initial public offering (IPO) on April 12, 1996. The IPO marked a pivotal moment in the company's history, transforming it from a fledgling startup into a publicly traded tech giant. Yahoo!'s stock debuted at $13 per share, and within minutes, it soared to over $30, signaling the market's excitement about the company's potential.

The IPO raised over $33 million, giving Yahoo! the capital it needed to continue its aggressive expansion and invest in new products. The company's valuation continued to climb throughout the late 1990s, especially during the dot-com boom, when tech stocks were reaching unprecedented heights. By 1999, Yahoo! was one of the most valuable companies in the world, with its stock price exceeding $100 per share at its peak.

This financial success allowed Yahoo! to make high-profile acquisitions, including the purchase of GeoCities (a web hosting service) and Broadcast.com (a streaming media company), further expanding its reach. Yahoo! was riding high, with both investors and users seeing it as the future of the internet.

The Dot-Com Boom: Yahoo!'s Meteoric Rise

The late 1990s were marked by the explosive growth of internet companies, and Yahoo! was at the forefront of this revolution. As more people gained access to the internet, Yahoo! benefited from the surge in new users. During this time, the company's stock price reached astronomical levels, and Yahoo! became a symbol of the dot-com boom—a period characterized by intense speculation, massive investment in internet companies, and a belief that the internet would transform every aspect of life.

Yahoo! capitalized on this boom by continually expanding its services and global presence. It launched country-specific versions of its site, including Yahoo! Japan and Yahoo! Europe, and it began offering services in multiple languages, making it a truly global platform. Yahoo!'s global expansion helped it capture markets across Asia, Europe, and the Americas, further solidifying its dominance.

By the end of the decade, Yahoo! had become one of the most visited websites in the world, with millions of users logging in daily to check their email, read the news, and explore the internet. It was crowned the "king of the web," and its position as the leading internet portal seemed unassailable.

Yahoo!'s Dominance: A Snapshot of Success

By 1999, Yahoo! was the internet's undisputed leader. It boasted hundreds of millions of users worldwide, and its wide array of services made it indispensable to everyday internet users. Yahoo!'s business model, which relied heavily on advertising revenue, was highly profitable, and the company's ability to attract advertisers from across industries cemented its financial success.

Yahoo! became more than just a search engine or web directory; it was an ecosystem where users could do everything from sending emails to checking stock prices. The brand was everywhere, from magazine ads to television commercials, and it represented the new digital age for many people. Yahoo!'s iconic "Yodel" jingle became a symbol of the internet's promise and excitement.

Conclusion: Yahoo!'s High-Water Mark

As the 1990s came to a close, Yahoo! stood at the pinnacle of the internet world. It was a pioneering force, shaping how millions of people experienced the web. Yahoo! had successfully transitioned from a simple directory into a multifaceted internet portal, offering services that touched on nearly every aspect of online life. Its influence was vast, its user base was growing, and its stock was soaring.

However, behind the scenes, challenges were beginning to mount. New competitors were emerging, and the internet was evolving faster than anyone could have anticipated.

While Yahoo! was riding high in 1999, the dawn of a new millennium would bring new trials and tribulations that would test the company's ability to maintain its dominance.

Chapter 3: The Dot-Com Bubble and Yahoo!'s First Fall

At the dawn of the internet age in the mid-1990s, technology companies were the golden children of the stock market, and investors scrambled to buy into the burgeoning dot-com sector. Yahoo! was one of the brightest stars in this new galaxy, and as internet penetration grew rapidly, the company's stock price skyrocketed. Yahoo!'s ascent coincided with an era of speculative investing, where the mere mention of an internet business could propel a company's valuation to stratospheric heights. Yahoo! embodied the exuberance of this period, and by the late 1990s, it had become a symbol of the internet boom.

However, this meteoric rise was built on a fragile foundation—overvaluation, over-optimism, and a lack of clear profitability strategies across the tech sector. As the dot-com bubble continued to inflate, warning signs were ignored. The bubble eventually burst in 2000, unleashing one of the most significant economic crashes in modern history, and Yahoo! was one of the companies caught in the wreckage. This chapter examines Yahoo!'s role in the dot-com bubble, the fallout from the burst, and the company's attempts to rebound in an increasingly competitive digital landscape.

The Rise Before the Fall: Yahoo! at the Height of the Dot-Com Boom

By 1999, Yahoo! was riding high on the wave of the dot-com bubble. The company's stock price soared as investors poured money into internet-based businesses, many of which had little more than a vague promise of future profitability. Yahoo!, at least, had a clear user base—its website was one of the most visited on the internet, and services like Yahoo! Mail, Yahoo! News, and Yahoo! Finance were attracting millions of users worldwide. The company had successfully branded itself as a gateway to the internet, positioning itself as a central hub for both consumers and advertisers.

Yahoo! capitalized on this popularity by rapidly expanding its offerings. It made several acquisitions, from online communication services to early search engine technologies, in an effort to dominate as much of the web as possible. These investments seemed sound in the short term, and Yahoo!'s revenue grew, largely driven by advertising and partnerships. The company's stock price reflected this optimism, reaching an all-time high of $237.50 per share in January 2000, giving Yahoo! a market capitalization of over $100 billion. At its peak, Yahoo! was one of the most valuable companies on the planet.

Despite the optimism surrounding Yahoo!, there were cracks beneath the surface. Much of Yahoo!'s business model was tied to the online advertising market, which itself was in its infancy. While online ads brought in substantial revenue, the returns were uncertain, and Yahoo! had yet to figure out how to translate its massive user base into sustained, long-term profitability. The company, like many others during the dot-com boom, was relying more on its stock price and investor confidence than on sound financial fundamentals.

The Dot-Com Bubble Bursts: 2000 and the Fall of Yahoo!

The first signs of trouble emerged in early 2000 when several high-profile internet companies began to falter, exposing the inflated valuations that had come to define the dot-com era. As it became clear that many dot-com companies lacked viable business models, investor confidence wavered, and a panic began to spread. In March 2000, the NASDAQ Composite Index, which had been heavily driven by tech stocks, began its precipitous decline, marking the start of the dot-com crash.

Yahoo!, once the poster child of internet success, saw its stock plummet. From its peak in January 2000, Yahoo!'s share price collapsed by over 90% within two years, falling to just $10.94 in September 2001. The company's market capitalization, which had once exceeded $100 billion, shrank to a fraction of that value. The sudden and dramatic fall in stock price was not just a reflection of Yahoo!'s overvaluation, but also of the broader correction that was taking place across the technology sector. Investors who had once clamored to buy into Yahoo! and other tech companies were now fleeing, and the entire internet industry entered a period of retrenchment.

Yahoo!'s Response: Diversification and New Ventures

In the wake of the crash, Yahoo! scrambled to find a way to reverse its fortunes. The company's leadership understood that simply relying on advertising revenue would no longer suffice, especially as businesses across the tech industry tightened their belts in the face of the market correction. In response, Yahoo! embarked on a strategy of diversification, attempting to branch out into new areas in hopes of stabilizing the company's revenue streams.

One of Yahoo!'s key moves was to push further into the realm of communication with the expansion of **Yahoo! Messenger**, a real-time chat service that gained significant popularity during the early 2000s. Yahoo! Messenger allowed users to communicate via text and later incorporated voice and video chat features. It became one of the first widely used messaging services, competing with platforms like AOL Instant Messenger. While Yahoo! Messenger attracted millions of users, it didn't provide the kind of revenue growth Yahoo! needed to replace its dwindling advertising dollars.

Another attempt at diversification came with **Yahoo! Auctions**, an effort to compete with eBay in the lucrative online auction space. Yahoo! Auctions was launched in several countries and offered a fee-free platform for users to buy and sell goods. Despite early excitement, Yahoo! Auctions struggled to gain traction in key markets, particularly in the U.S., where eBay had already established itself as the dominant player. The lack of a clear differentiation from eBay made it difficult for Yahoo! to capture market share, and the venture was eventually phased out in most regions.

The company also invested in **Yahoo! Stores**, an e-commerce platform that allowed small businesses to create and manage online storefronts. This move was intended to capture some of the growing e-commerce market, which was rapidly expanding with the rise of companies like Amazon. However, Yahoo! Stores never achieved the scale or success that was anticipated, largely due to stiff competition from other platforms that were more nimble and user-friendly.

Despite these efforts, Yahoo!'s diversification strategy lacked a coherent focus. The company was trying to compete in too many areas simultaneously—messaging, auctions, e-commerce, media—and was spread too thin to achieve dominance in any one sector. The lack of a clear, unified strategy meant that many of these ventures failed to deliver the necessary results, and Yahoo!'s financial situation remained precarious.

The Rise of Google: A New Era of Search Dominance

While Yahoo! was grappling with the aftermath of the dot-com crash, a new player was quietly revolutionizing the world of internet search: **Google**. Founded in 1998, Google had a simple mission—provide the best search results as quickly as possible. Unlike Yahoo!, which had evolved into a portal with a broad range of services, Google was singularly focused on refining its search algorithms to deliver faster, more relevant results.

Yahoo!'s initial response to Google's rise was one of complacency. The company believed that its broad array of services, combined with its brand recognition, would be enough to maintain its lead in the search market. However, by the early 2000s, it became clear that users were increasingly turning to Google for their search needs. Google's PageRank algorithm, which ranked websites based on relevance and importance, was far superior to the directory-based search model Yahoo! had pioneered.

In 2000, Yahoo! made a critical decision: it outsourced its search engine results to Google. At the time, this may have seemed like a practical solution—Google's search technology was more advanced, and Yahoo! could still retain its role as a portal. However, this decision would prove to be a major strategic misstep. By relying on Google for search, Yahoo! essentially handed over the most valuable piece of the internet ecosystem—search—and allowed its competitor to gain a foothold in the market.

By the mid-2000s, Google had become the undisputed leader in internet search, and its advertising platform, **Google AdWords**, was revolutionizing the way companies approached online marketing. Yahoo!, once the king of the web, was now struggling to keep pace. The rise of Google marked a profound shift in the balance of power in the tech world, and Yahoo!'s inability to compete effectively in the search space would haunt the company for years to come.

Conclusion: Yahoo!'s Struggles in the Post-Bubble World

The dot-com crash marked a turning point for Yahoo! and the broader internet industry. While Yahoo! survived the collapse of the bubble, it emerged from the wreckage a weakened company, burdened by failed diversification efforts and facing stiff competition from more focused and innovative rivals like Google. The early 2000s were a time of soul-searching for Yahoo!, as the company struggled to find a new direction and adapt to a rapidly changing internet landscape.

The rise of Google signaled the end of Yahoo!'s dominance in the search market, and the company's attempts to branch out into new areas—messaging, auctions, and e-commerce—ultimately fell short. The lack of a coherent strategy, combined with the fallout from the dot-com crash, left Yahoo! vulnerable, and the company's glory days seemed to be behind it.

However, as the story of Yahoo! would later show, this was not the end of the company's journey. Despite its challenges, Yahoo! would continue to evolve, and its story of resilience and reinvention was far from over.

Chapter 4: Missed Opportunities – Google, Facebook, and the Deals That Never Happened

In the world of technology, timing is often everything, and the ability to foresee future trends can make or break a company. Yahoo!, once a trailblazer of the internet, found itself at several crossroads where key decisions could have dramatically altered its fate. However, the company's failure to seize critical opportunities with emerging tech giants, particularly Google and Facebook, stands as one of the most infamous cautionary tales in Silicon Valley history.

The Google Deal – A $1 Billion Mistake

One of the most crucial moments in Yahoo!'s history occurred in the late 1990s when it had the chance to acquire a fledgling company that would go on to dominate the internet—Google.

Google, founded by Larry Page and Sergey Brin in 1998, was not immediately recognized as the groundbreaking search engine that it would later become. In fact, Google's founders originally developed their search algorithm while at Stanford University, hoping to license it to existing search engines. At the time, Yahoo! was one of the leaders in search, using an early directory-based system to organize websites and help users navigate the internet. Its search engine was powered by third-party technology, and Yahoo! primarily focused on being a portal for news, email, and various web services rather than a search-centric platform.

By 1998, Page and Brin approached Yahoo! with the idea of selling their company for around $1 billion. Yahoo! executives, however, were not interested. They believed that their existing search technology—combined with the portal structure they had built—was sufficient. Moreover, Yahoo! viewed itself as more than just a search engine. It was becoming a full-service internet destination with services like Yahoo! Mail, Yahoo! Finance, and Yahoo! News.

Yahoo!'s leadership team saw the internet through a different lens: search was just one component, and their belief was that users would prefer a single destination that offered everything rather than a specialized service like Google's search algorithm. The executives also feared that acquiring Google would disrupt Yahoo!'s carefully curated user experience. This decision reflected a broader underestimation of how powerful and important search would become in the digital economy.

However, as the internet continued to expand and websites multiplied, it became clear that directory-based search systems like Yahoo!'s were struggling to keep pace. Google's search engine, built on its PageRank algorithm, proved to be far superior in organizing the vast and rapidly growing web. It offered faster, more relevant search results and quickly gained a loyal user base. Google's clean, minimalist homepage, focused solely on search, stood in stark contrast to Yahoo!'s increasingly cluttered portal.

Yahoo!'s failure to acquire Google would become one of the biggest missed opportunities in tech history. By the early 2000s, Google had not only surpassed Yahoo! as the world's most popular search engine but also became the dominant player in digital advertising. Google's AdWords platform revolutionized online advertising, giving the company a massive revenue stream. By the time Yahoo! realized the extent of its mistake, it was too late—Google had grown into an untouchable tech juggernaut.

The Second Chance: Another Missed Opportunity

In 2002, Yahoo! had another chance to acquire Google. This time, Google was already gaining significant momentum and had become a formidable player in search. Yahoo!'s then-CEO Terry Semel was reportedly interested in buying Google and offered $3 billion. By this point, however, Google's co-founders Larry Page and Sergey

Brin believed that their company was worth far more. They demanded $5 billion, but Yahoo! executives balked at the price. Once again, Yahoo! walked away from a deal that could have fundamentally changed the company's future.

In hindsight, the decision not to pay $5 billion for Google was a devastating blow to Yahoo!'s long-term competitiveness. Within just a few years, Google's market dominance exploded, and its market capitalization soared into the hundreds of billions. Yahoo! would never again have the opportunity to catch up in the search space, as Google solidified its role as the gateway to the internet.

The Facebook Acquisition That Never Was

If the Google story wasn't enough, Yahoo! found itself in a strikingly similar situation just a few years later with another emerging tech company—Facebook.

Founded by Mark Zuckerberg in 2004, Facebook started as a social networking platform for college students but quickly expanded to a broader audience. By 2006, Facebook had captured the attention of millions of users and was on the verge of exploding into mainstream culture. Yahoo!, seeing the rise of social media and the potential of Facebook, made a move to acquire the company.

At the time, Facebook was still a relatively small startup, and Zuckerberg was open to the idea of selling the company. Yahoo! approached Zuckerberg with an offer of $1 billion, a significant sum for a two-year-old company. By all accounts, Zuckerberg was seriously considering the offer, and many in his circle believed that the deal would go through.

However, just as negotiations were underway, Yahoo!'s stock price took a hit, causing its board to become jittery. Yahoo! executives, worried about their financial position, lowered their offer to $850 million. Zuckerberg, frustrated by the sudden change in terms, walked away from the deal. He believed in Facebook's potential and saw the reduced offer as a lack of faith in the company's future.

In the years that followed, Zuckerberg's decision to hold onto Facebook proved to be one of the most pivotal in tech history. Facebook grew exponentially, becoming the world's largest social network and fundamentally altering the way people communicate and interact online. It also became one of the most valuable companies in the world, with a market capitalization in the hundreds of billions.

For Yahoo!, the failed acquisition of Facebook was another missed opportunity that solidified its decline. By the time Facebook went public in 2012, Yahoo! was no longer in a position to compete with the new generation of tech giants, which included Facebook, Google, and Amazon.

What Could Have Been – The Impact of These Missed Opportunities

The missed acquisitions of Google and Facebook represent two of the most critical turning points in Yahoo!'s history. Had Yahoo! successfully acquired either company, it would have fundamentally changed the landscape of the internet. Acquiring Google in its early days could have made Yahoo! the undisputed leader in search and digital advertising, while owning Facebook would have given Yahoo! a foothold in the rapidly growing social media space.

Instead, Yahoo! found itself increasingly outmatched by these younger, more agile competitors. Google dominated search and advertising, while Facebook revolutionized social media and digital marketing. As Yahoo! struggled to maintain its relevance, these companies soared to unprecedented heights, becoming pillars of the modern internet.

Lessons Learned

The stories of Yahoo!, Google, and Facebook offer valuable lessons about the importance of vision, timing, and the ability to adapt. Yahoo! had the chance to acquire two of the most important companies in internet history, but its hesitation and short-term thinking led to missed opportunities. The reluctance to invest in emerging technologies or take bold risks often stifles innovation, a lesson Yahoo! learned the hard way.

In contrast, companies like Google and Facebook succeeded because they were not afraid to challenge the status quo and embrace new technologies. Their founders had a clear vision of the future, and they were willing to take risks to achieve it.

For Yahoo!, the missed acquisitions of Google and Facebook are more than just business deals that fell through—they are emblematic of the company's broader struggles with innovation and strategic decision-making. As a result, Yahoo! went from being one of the early pioneers of the internet to a company that was constantly playing catch-up.

Conclusion

Yahoo!'s missed opportunities with Google and Facebook are two of the most well-known examples of Silicon Valley's what-could-have-been stories. These decisions shaped not only Yahoo!'s trajectory but also the future of the internet as we know it. Google and Facebook went on to become titans in their respective fields, while Yahoo! slowly faded from the spotlight.

Despite these missteps, Yahoo!'s role in the early days of the web cannot be discounted. It was a pioneer, a trailblazer that helped shape the internet, but its inability to capitalize on game-changing opportunities serves as a powerful reminder that in the fast-paced world of technology, even the most dominant companies can be left behind if they fail to see the future clearly.

Chapter 5: The Marissa Mayer Era – Trying to Steer the Ship

In 2012, Yahoo! was a company in turmoil. Once an undisputed leader in the internet world, it had fallen dramatically behind its competitors. The company had experienced a series of leadership changes, with several CEOs coming and going in quick succession. These leaders struggled to develop a clear vision to reverse Yahoo!'s decline, and the company was losing ground to rapidly growing competitors like Google, Facebook, and Amazon.

Then, in July 2012, Yahoo! made headlines by appointing Marissa Mayer as its new CEO. At just 37 years old, Mayer was a high-profile executive with an impressive track record at Google, where she had been one of the company's first 20 employees. Mayer's appointment marked a significant moment in Yahoo!'s history, as the company placed its hopes on her leadership to revitalize its fortunes and re-establish itself as a major player in the tech world.

A Bold New Leader: Who Is Marissa Mayer?

Before delving into Mayer's tenure at Yahoo!, it's important to understand her background. Marissa Mayer joined Google in 1999 as the company's first female engineer and quickly rose through the ranks, eventually holding senior positions overseeing product development, user experience, and search. Mayer played a key role in many of Google's most successful products, including Google Search, Gmail, Google Maps, and Google News. She was known for her attention to detail, her focus on design and user experience, and her ability to manage large teams working on complex products.

Mayer's success at Google made her one of the most prominent figures in Silicon Valley, and her move to Yahoo! was seen as a major coup for the struggling company. Many analysts believed that Mayer had the skills, experience, and star power to turn Yahoo! around and make it competitive again in a tech landscape increasingly dominated by Google, Facebook, and Amazon.

Acquisition Strategy: Growth Through Buying Power

One of the central strategies Mayer employed to revive Yahoo! was aggressive acquisition. During her tenure, Mayer oversaw more than 50 acquisitions, aiming to bring in new talent, technology, and products to bolster Yahoo!'s portfolio. The most high-profile of these acquisitions was the purchase of Tumblr, the popular blogging platform, for $1.1 billion in 2013. Tumblr was particularly appealing because of its young, engaged user base, and Mayer hoped to use the platform to make Yahoo! more relevant to a younger demographic that was increasingly moving away from traditional web portals like Yahoo!.

Other notable acquisitions under Mayer's leadership included Summly, a news aggregation app founded by a teenager, and Flurry, a mobile analytics company. Mayer also acquired mobile apps like Aviate, a contextual homescreen app for Android, and Qwiki, a video creation app. The goal behind these purchases was to help Yahoo! pivot toward mobile technology, as Mayer recognized that the future of the internet was increasingly mobile-first.

Despite the boldness of Mayer's acquisition strategy, many of the purchases failed to deliver the desired results. Tumblr, in particular, became emblematic of Yahoo!'s struggles. While the acquisition initially generated excitement, Yahoo! struggled to monetize the platform, and its user base began to stagnate. Internal cultural clashes between Tumblr and Yahoo! employees also hindered the integration process, and in 2016, Yahoo! was forced to write down the value of Tumblr by $230 million. Tumblr's rapid decline, alongside other unsuccessful acquisitions, led to criticism of Mayer's strategy, with some accusing her of focusing on flashy purchases instead of long-term growth.

Focus on Mobile: A Shift in Strategy

Mayer was keenly aware that Yahoo! needed to adapt to the mobile revolution. At the time of her appointment, Yahoo! was still primarily focused on desktop services, despite the clear shift in consumer behavior toward smartphones and tablets. Under Mayer's leadership, Yahoo! made significant investments in mobile technology, launching new apps and redesigning existing services to be more mobile-friendly.

One of Mayer's first major initiatives was to revamp Yahoo!'s core apps, including Yahoo! Mail, Yahoo! Weather, and Yahoo! News Digest. The goal was to create streamlined, visually appealing mobile apps that would draw users back to Yahoo! and increase engagement. Yahoo! also placed a strong emphasis on mobile advertising, recognizing that this was a key area where Google and Facebook were far ahead.

Mayer's mobile push showed some initial success. By 2014, Yahoo! reported that its mobile apps had over 450 million monthly active users, a significant increase from the previous years. However, despite this progress, Yahoo! still lagged far behind its competitors in both user numbers and mobile ad revenue. Google and Facebook had a stranglehold on the mobile ad market, leaving Yahoo! struggling to carve out a significant share.

Product Redesigns: Streamlining Yahoo!'s Offerings

In addition to acquisitions and mobile expansion, Mayer embarked on an ambitious plan to redesign and modernize many of Yahoo!'s existing products. One of her key achievements was the overhaul of Yahoo!'s iconic homepage, which had become cluttered and outdated. Mayer's redesign aimed to make the homepage more personalized and user-friendly, with features like infinite scrolling and algorithm-driven content recommendations.

Yahoo! Mail also received a major update during Mayer's tenure. Mayer introduced a cleaner, more modern interface, along with new features like conversations view and disposable email addresses. The goal was to make Yahoo! Mail competitive with Gmail, which had become the dominant email provider by that point. Despite the improvements, Yahoo! Mail struggled to regain significant market share, as many users had already migrated to Gmail or other services.

Yahoo! Finance and Yahoo! Sports, two of the company's most successful products, also saw updates under Mayer's leadership. Yahoo! Finance introduced new tools for investors, while Yahoo! Sports expanded its coverage and introduced features like live sports streaming and fantasy sports integration. These efforts helped to maintain Yahoo!'s strong position in these areas, but they weren't enough to offset the company's broader struggles.

Cultural and Internal Challenges: A Divided Workforce

One of Mayer's biggest challenges as CEO was navigating Yahoo!'s internal culture. The company had become bloated and bureaucratic, with many employees feeling disengaged and demoralized after years of leadership changes and declining performance. Mayer implemented a number of changes aimed at revitalizing Yahoo!'s culture, including eliminating the company's work-from-home policy in an effort to foster more collaboration and innovation.

This decision, however, sparked significant backlash both internally and externally. Many employees, particularly those with family commitments, viewed the policy change as a step backward in terms of work-life balance. Additionally, some felt that Mayer's leadership style— described by some as micromanaging—fostered an environment of fear and uncertainty, further hampering employee morale.

Despite these challenges, Mayer did succeed in attracting top talent to Yahoo!. Many former Google employees followed her to Yahoo!, bringing with them fresh ideas and expertise. However, even with these new hires, Yahoo!'s internal struggles persisted, and the company continued to face difficulties in executing its strategies.

The Struggle to Compete: Yahoo!'s Place in a New Tech World

One of the fundamental problems Mayer faced was that Yahoo! had been left behind by its competitors in key areas of the tech world. Google had become synonymous with search, Facebook had taken over social media, and Amazon was quickly becoming a dominant force in e-commerce and cloud computing. Yahoo!, by contrast, was still heavily reliant on its legacy products, like Yahoo! Mail and Yahoo! Finance, which were losing relevance in an increasingly mobile and data-driven internet landscape.

Mayer's efforts to pivot Yahoo! toward mobile, content, and advertising were not enough to close the gap with its competitors. Despite making improvements to its core products and acquiring new companies, Yahoo! simply could not match the scale, innovation, and growth of tech giants like Google and Facebook.

Final Years of Mayer's Tenure: Financial Stabilization but Limited Growth

While Mayer's tenure was marked by ambitious initiatives, it ultimately failed to deliver the kind of turnaround that many had hoped for. Yahoo!'s stock price did see a significant rise during Mayer's time as CEO, but much of this increase was driven by Yahoo!'s stake in Alibaba, the Chinese e-commerce giant. Yahoo! had invested in

Alibaba years earlier, and as Alibaba's value skyrocketed, so did Yahoo!'s stock. However, this financial boost was largely unrelated to Yahoo!'s core business operations.

In 2016, after years of declining revenues and shrinking market share, Yahoo! announced that it would sell its core internet business to Verizon for $4.8 billion. The sale marked the end of Yahoo! as an independent company and the culmination of Mayer's efforts to stabilize the company. While Mayer was able to prevent Yahoo! from completely collapsing, she was ultimately unable to restore it to its former glory.

Legacy of the Marissa Mayer Era

Marissa Mayer's time at Yahoo! is often viewed as a mixed bag. On one hand, she brought much-needed energy, vision, and leadership to a company that had been floundering for years. Her focus on mobile, product redesigns, and acquisitions helped to modernize Yahoo! and make it more relevant in a rapidly changing tech landscape.

On the other hand, many of her initiatives failed to deliver the long-term results that Yahoo! needed. The acquisition strategy, while bold, did not generate the kind of growth Mayer had hoped for, and internal cultural challenges continued to plague the company. Ultimately, Mayer was unable to compete effectively with Google, Facebook, and Amazon, and Yahoo! remained a shadow of its former self.

Mayer's legacy at Yahoo! is a cautionary tale about the difficulties of turning around a once-dominant tech company in a highly competitive and fast-moving industry. Despite her best efforts, Yahoo! was never able to regain its position as a leader in the internet world, and its eventual sale to Verizon marked the end of an era for one of Silicon Valley's original giants.

Chapter 6: The Verizon Acquisition – A New Era for Yahoo!

The year 2016 marked a pivotal turning point in the history of Yahoo!, a company that had once been a trailblazer in the early internet era. After years of financial struggles, missed opportunities, and failed attempts to regain its former dominance, Yahoo! made headlines once again—not for a revival of its fortunes, but for its acquisition by telecommunications giant Verizon. The $4.8 billion deal represented the end of Yahoo! as an independent entity, capping off a dramatic decline from its once-lofty position as one of the internet's pioneers.

For Verizon, this acquisition was more than just a purchase—it was part of a broader strategy to build a powerful media and advertising platform by integrating Yahoo! with another internet relic, AOL. Verizon's hope was that by combining the two companies, it could challenge the dominance of Google and Facebook in the digital advertising space. This chapter takes a deep dive into the intricacies of the acquisition, the subsequent changes within Yahoo!, and how Verizon's ambitions reshaped the company's future.

The Road to Acquisition

By 2016, Yahoo! was a company in distress. Years of declining market share in search and advertising, compounded by intense competition from Google, Facebook, and other digital powerhouses, had eroded its value. While Yahoo! still had millions of users across its services like Yahoo! Mail, Yahoo! Finance, and Yahoo! Sports, the company was no longer the innovator it once was.

Yahoo! had also suffered significant leadership turbulence, with multiple CEOs attempting, and failing, to reinvigorate the company. In 2012, Marissa Mayer, a former Google executive, was brought in as CEO to steer Yahoo! in a new direction. Mayer's tenure saw some successes, including the growth of Yahoo!'s mobile user base and various high-profile acquisitions, such as the $1.1 billion purchase of Tumblr. However, Mayer's grand vision for Yahoo! never fully materialized. The company continued to lose relevance, and the looming threat of data breaches (two of which would eventually be revealed during the acquisition process) further undermined public trust.

After several attempts to find a suitable buyer, in July 2016, Yahoo! agreed to sell its core internet operations to Verizon for $4.8 billion. This acquisition excluded Yahoo!'s valuable stakes in Alibaba Group and Yahoo!

Japan, which were held in a separate entity called Altaba, and would later be liquidated. The sale marked the end of Yahoo! as a stand-alone company and a public entity, though the Yahoo! brand and its services would continue under new ownership.

Verizon's Vision: Merging Yahoo! and AOL

Verizon's acquisition of Yahoo! was not a standalone purchase but part of a larger strategy. Verizon had acquired AOL in 2015 for $4.4 billion, and with Yahoo!'s addition, Verizon aimed to create a formidable digital media and advertising company that could compete with Google and Facebook. The combined assets of Yahoo! and AOL offered Verizon a broad portfolio of online properties, including Yahoo! News, Yahoo! Sports, AOL's Huffington Post, and the advertising technology platforms of both companies.

Verizon merged Yahoo! and AOL into a new division called Oath. The goal was to leverage Yahoo!'s popular services, such as Yahoo! Mail, Yahoo! Finance, and Yahoo! Sports, alongside AOL's media brands to build a comprehensive media ecosystem. Oath aimed to capitalize on Yahoo!'s vast user base, which still numbered in the hundreds of millions, and its extensive data for targeted advertising.

Oath was expected to serve as Verizon's entry point into the highly competitive digital advertising space, a market dominated by Google and Facebook. Verizon believed that the combination of Yahoo! and AOL's ad technologies would allow Oath to become a significant player in digital advertising, particularly in programmatic advertising, which uses automation to target ads to specific users based on data.

Yahoo! Under Oath: Changes and Challenges

The formation of Oath was intended to be a fresh start for Yahoo!, but the integration of two legacy internet companies with different cultures and histories was far from smooth. Yahoo! and AOL, once fierce competitors, were now expected to work together under the Verizon umbrella. The ambitious plans for Oath faced several immediate challenges.

One of the most significant obstacles was the revelation of two massive data breaches that occurred under Yahoo!'s watch. In late 2016, just after the acquisition was announced, Yahoo! disclosed that over 1 billion user accounts had been compromised in a 2013 data breach, followed by a separate breach affecting 500 million accounts in 2014. These breaches were some of the largest in internet history, and their disclosure cast a shadow over the acquisition, resulting in Verizon renegotiating the final sale price, reducing it by $350 million. The breaches also led to lawsuits, regulatory scrutiny, and a major loss of user trust, tarnishing Yahoo!'s reputation even further.

Despite these challenges, the core Yahoo! services— Yahoo! Mail, Yahoo! Finance, and Yahoo! Sports— remained popular. These products had loyal user bases and continued to attract millions of visitors. Yahoo! Mail, in particular, was a key asset, with over 225 million users at the time of the acquisition, making it one of the largest email platforms in the world. Yahoo! Finance had become a go-to destination for financial news and stock market data, while Yahoo! Sports maintained a strong presence, particularly in the fantasy sports market.

However, Oath struggled to make a significant impact in the digital advertising market. Despite its considerable content and data assets, it could not match the scale and precision of Google and Facebook's advertising platforms. The competitive pressure from these tech giants, along with the challenge of integrating Yahoo! and AOL's technologies, led to internal restructuring and layoffs at Oath.

Rebranding as Verizon Media: A New Approach

In 2018, just two years after the creation of Oath, Verizon decided to rebrand the division as Verizon Media, marking the end of the Oath name. The rebranding was part of

Verizon's broader strategy to focus on its core strengths in telecommunications while maintaining a presence in digital media and advertising.

Under the Verizon Media banner, Yahoo! continued to operate as a brand, with its most prominent services— Yahoo! Mail, Yahoo! Finance, and Yahoo! Sports— remaining integral parts of the company's offering. Verizon shifted its focus from challenging Google and Facebook head-on in the advertising space to maximizing the value of its existing assets, particularly in content and user engagement.

Yahoo! Finance, for instance, became a centerpiece of Verizon Media's strategy, offering premium financial news and data services, expanding its video content, and hosting live events like the Yahoo! Finance All Markets Summit. Yahoo! Sports continued to grow its fantasy sports offerings and partnered with major sports leagues, while Yahoo! Mail received updates to improve user experience and privacy features.

Verizon Media also invested in new technologies like 5G to enhance its digital media services and explore innovative advertising formats. However, Verizon's ambitions for its media division never fully materialized, and the company continued to face challenges in monetizing its vast content and user base.

The End of Verizon's Media Experiment: Apollo Global Management

In May 2021, Verizon announced that it had sold Verizon Media, including Yahoo! and AOL, to private equity firm Apollo Global Management for $5 billion. The sale marked the end of Verizon's foray into the digital media business, with the company shifting its focus back to its telecommunications roots. Apollo rebranded the media division simply as "Yahoo!" signaling a renewed focus on revitalizing the Yahoo! brand.

This transition marked another chapter in Yahoo!'s long and tumultuous history. Under Apollo's ownership, Yahoo! was given the opportunity to operate more independently and strategically, with a focus on its core businesses in email, finance, sports, and content. While Yahoo! was no longer the dominant internet player it once was, it continued to serve millions of loyal users and remained a relevant, albeit smaller, part of the digital media landscape.

Conclusion: A New Era for Yahoo!

The Verizon acquisition and subsequent transition to Apollo ownership represent a new era for Yahoo!, one defined by reinvention and adaptation. Although Yahoo! is no longer the internet giant it was in the late 1990s and early 2000s, it has found a way to remain relevant by focusing on its core strengths. Services like Yahoo! Mail, Yahoo! Finance, and Yahoo! Sports have continued to thrive, maintaining a strong user base and evolving to meet the needs of a changing internet landscape.

The Verizon acquisition, while not the game-changer many had hoped for, gave Yahoo! a lifeline and allowed it to continue operating as a trusted brand in the digital space. Now, under Apollo's ownership, Yahoo! has the opportunity to reinvent itself once again, proving that even in the fast-paced world of technology, there is always room for reinvention.

Yahoo!'s story is a testament to the challenges of staying relevant in the ever-evolving tech world, but it also highlights the resilience of a brand that, despite many ups and downs, has remained a fixture in the lives of millions of internet users.

Chapter 7: Reinventing Yahoo! – The Path Forward

Though Yahoo! may no longer dominate the internet as it did in its heyday, the company has proven that it is far from obsolete. The acquisition by Verizon in 2017 marked a turning point for Yahoo!, allowing it to restructure and refocus its efforts on its strongest, most enduring services: Yahoo! Finance, Yahoo! Sports, and Yahoo! Mail. These platforms have provided a solid foundation for the company as it reinvents itself in an increasingly competitive and rapidly evolving digital landscape. This chapter explores Yahoo!'s strategic reinvention, its renewed focus on core services, and its continued relevance in today's tech world.

A Strategic Refocus on Strengths

Following years of missed opportunities, unsuccessful acquisitions, and struggles to compete with newer, more nimble tech giants, Yahoo! found itself at a crossroads by the mid-2010s. Verizon's acquisition gave Yahoo! the financial backing and organizational support needed to reimagine its role in the online ecosystem. The once sprawling web portal that had tried to offer everything to everyone began to narrow its focus, honing in on the areas where it still had considerable value: finance, sports, and email.

Yahoo!'s decision to concentrate on its most popular services was a key step in its reinvention. These three core areas—Yahoo! Finance, Yahoo! Sports, and Yahoo! Mail—had consistently retained strong user bases, even as other Yahoo! services faltered. The company recognized that, rather than competing directly with tech behemoths like Google, Facebook, and Amazon in areas such as search and social media, it could still thrive by doubling down on its niche markets where it had proven expertise and brand loyalty.

Yahoo! Finance: The Go-To Platform for Financial News and Tools

Among Yahoo!'s most enduring assets is Yahoo! Finance. Established in 1997, Yahoo! Finance quickly became a trusted source for financial news, data, and analysis, particularly for retail investors and everyday consumers seeking accessible, real-time market information. As Yahoo! shifted its priorities post-acquisition, Yahoo! Finance emerged as one of the crown jewels of the company's portfolio, and it has continued to evolve as a major player in the world of digital finance.

One of the key factors behind Yahoo! Finance's ongoing success has been its ability to blend high-quality financial journalism with real-time stock market data and analytical tools. Users can access everything from breaking news about major companies and economic trends to detailed stock charts, portfolio management tools, and financial analysis. The platform's ease of use has allowed it to remain popular among both novice investors and seasoned professionals alike.

In recent years, Yahoo! Finance has taken advantage of the growing interest in stock market participation, fueled by trends such as the rise of retail investing and the popularity of platforms like Robinhood. Recognizing this shift, Yahoo! Finance has expanded its offerings to include live video broadcasts, featuring expert commentary and analysis on market movements, as well as in-depth reporting on the latest trends in cryptocurrency, fintech, and global economics.

Additionally, Yahoo! Finance has capitalized on the explosion of financial content creators and influencers, further strengthening its position as a hub for both professional and user-generated financial content. By maintaining its commitment to providing reliable data and insightful analysis, Yahoo! Finance has managed to stay relevant in a crowded market where other financial news platforms have come and gone.

Yahoo! Sports: The Fantasy Sports Giant

Another pillar of Yahoo!'s reinvention strategy has been Yahoo! Sports, which remains a top destination for sports enthusiasts. Originally launched in 1997 as a part of Yahoo!'s expansive web portal, Yahoo! Sports has consistently adapted to the evolving needs of sports fans, particularly in the realm of fantasy sports.

Yahoo! was one of the first major internet companies to dive into the world of fantasy sports, launching its fantasy football platform in 1999. Since then, Yahoo! Fantasy Sports has grown to cover not just football, but also baseball, basketball, and hockey, attracting millions of users who rely on the platform to manage their fantasy leagues and track player stats. The platform's user-friendly interface and advanced features, such as real-time updates, draft tools, and expert advice, have helped cement Yahoo! Fantasy Sports as a leader in the industry.

One of the major reasons Yahoo! Sports has remained relevant is its focus on community engagement. Fantasy sports, by nature, are social experiences, and Yahoo! has built its platform around fostering connections between players through message boards, chat features, and custom leagues. This emphasis on user interaction has kept Yahoo! Fantasy Sports competitive, even as newer fantasy platforms, such as ESPN Fantasy and DraftKings, entered the market.

In recent years, Yahoo! has continued to innovate within the fantasy sports space, offering daily and weekly fantasy contests, as well as partnering with major sports leagues to provide exclusive content and experiences. Yahoo! Sports has also expanded into sports betting, recognizing the growing demand for legalized betting in the U.S. and incorporating betting odds, insights, and tips into its platform.

Yahoo! Mail: Reliable Communication in a Mobile World

While Yahoo! Mail may not be as innovative or groundbreaking as it was when it launched in 1997, it remains one of the most widely used email services in the world. With hundreds of millions of active users, Yahoo! Mail has maintained its relevance by focusing on reliability, security, and user-friendly design.

Yahoo! Mail's mobile app, in particular, has helped the platform stay competitive in a world where mobile communication dominates. The app offers a clean, intuitive interface, and includes features such as customizable themes, multiple email account integration, and advanced spam filtering. For users who value simplicity and consistency in their email experience, Yahoo! Mail remains a trusted option.

Yahoo! has also prioritized security in response to growing concerns about data breaches and online privacy. After facing a major data breach in 2013, which affected billions of user accounts, Yahoo! implemented significant security enhancements, including two-factor authentication, end-to-end encryption, and AI-driven spam detection. These improvements have helped restore user confidence and ensure that Yahoo! Mail remains a reliable option for personal and business communication.

The Road to Reinvention: Challenges and Opportunities

While Yahoo! has successfully stabilized its position in the digital landscape, the company continues to face significant challenges. The tech industry moves at an extraordinary pace, and Yahoo! must continue to innovate and adapt to remain competitive. The rise of artificial intelligence (AI), machine learning, and personalized user experiences poses both opportunities and threats to Yahoo!'s core services.

In particular, Yahoo! will need to leverage emerging technologies to enhance its offerings in finance, sports, and email. Personalized financial insights powered by AI, enhanced data analytics for fantasy sports players, and smarter email organization systems are just a few areas where Yahoo! could apply its resources to stay ahead of the curve.

Moreover, as the digital media space becomes increasingly fragmented, Yahoo! must find ways to differentiate itself from competitors. Collaborating with major content creators, sports leagues, and financial institutions could help Yahoo! strengthen its position as a leading platform in its niche areas. By staying true to its strengths while embracing technological advancements, Yahoo! can continue to evolve and remain relevant in a crowded marketplace.

Conclusion: Yahoo!'s Enduring Legacy

Yahoo!'s path to reinvention has been defined by its ability to focus on what it does best. While it may no longer be the internet giant it once was, Yahoo! has carved out a sustainable role in the digital world by concentrating on its core strengths—finance, sports, and email. These services continue to attract millions of users who value Yahoo!'s long-standing reputation for reliability and innovation.

As Yahoo! continues its journey forward, its legacy as one of the internet's pioneers remains intact. The company's story is one of resilience, adaptability, and the recognition that, in the fast-paced world of technology, even giants must evolve. Through careful reinvention and a commitment to delivering high-quality user experiences,

Yahoo! has ensured that it remains a significant player in the online ecosystem. The road ahead may be uncertain, but Yahoo!'s ability to learn from its past and adapt to the future gives it the potential to thrive for years to come.

Chapter 8: Lessons from Yahoo! – The Rise and Fall of Internet Giants

Yahoo!'s story is emblematic of the rise and fall many tech companies experience in the fast-paced world of the internet. Born in an era when the internet was still a fledgling network, Yahoo! was one of the original pioneers of the online world, helping to shape how people navigated and interacted with websites. From its meteoric rise as a leading web portal to its eventual decline, Yahoo!'s trajectory highlights key lessons about innovation, foresight, and adaptability in the technology industry. This chapter examines the broader lessons that can be gleaned from Yahoo!'s journey, offering insights into how other internet giants can avoid similar pitfalls and stay relevant in an ever-changing digital landscape.

1. The Importance of Timing and Foresight

One of the most important lessons from Yahoo!'s history is the critical role that timing and foresight play in determining a company's success. In the early 1990s, Yahoo! was in the right place at the right time. The internet was rapidly growing, and there was a demand for a platform that could organize and categorize the increasing number of websites. Yahoo!'s web directory became a crucial tool for users, offering a simple, easy-to-use solution for navigating the vastness of the web.

However, as the internet evolved, so did users' needs. The rise of search engines, particularly Google, fundamentally changed how people accessed information online. Google's algorithm-based search, which prioritized relevance over simple directory listings, quickly outpaced Yahoo!'s directory model. Yahoo! failed to recognize the significance of Google's innovation and continued to invest in its directory-based approach even as the web shifted toward more efficient search mechanisms. The lesson here is that tech companies must not only innovate but also anticipate how market trends and user behavior will evolve.

Yahoo!'s failure to acquire Google when it had the chance underscores the importance of foresight in tech strategy. In 2002, Google was still a young company, and Yahoo! had the opportunity to purchase it for $1 billion. Yahoo! executives hesitated, believing that their own search capabilities were sufficient to compete. Google, of course, went on to dominate the search engine market, leaving Yahoo! in its shadow. This missed opportunity is now regarded as one of the biggest strategic missteps in tech history, illustrating that recognizing the potential of emerging competitors is crucial for long-term survival.

2. The Cost of Missed Opportunities

Yahoo!'s reluctance to seize critical opportunities extended beyond its failure to acquire Google. The company's history is marked by several other instances where it hesitated to make bold moves that could have reshaped its future.

In 2006, Yahoo! had another chance to stay ahead of the curve when it considered purchasing Facebook for $1 billion. At the time, Facebook was still an up-and-coming social media platform, and Yahoo! saw potential in adding it to its portfolio. However, when Yahoo! lowered its offer to $850 million, negotiations with Facebook's CEO, Mark Zuckerberg, broke down. Facebook would go on to revolutionize the internet and social networking, and its value would skyrocket to hundreds of billions of dollars. Once again, Yahoo! failed to act decisively, missing out on a transformative acquisition that could have positioned it as a leader in the next wave of internet innovation.

The lesson here is clear: In the fast-moving world of tech, hesitation can be costly. Companies must be willing to take calculated risks and recognize when an opportunity has the potential to change the landscape of the industry. Yahoo!'s indecisiveness allowed competitors like Google and Facebook to surpass it, ultimately relegating Yahoo! to the status of a follower rather than a leader in the internet space.

3. The Role of Innovation in Staying Competitive

Innovation is the lifeblood of the technology industry, and companies that fail to innovate are at risk of stagnation. Yahoo! was once seen as an innovative company, introducing popular services such as Yahoo! Mail, Yahoo! News, and Yahoo! Finance. However, as the internet continued to evolve, Yahoo! struggled to keep pace with the innovations of its competitors.

Google's development of a more efficient and user-friendly search engine, Facebook's creation of a global social media platform, and even Amazon's dominance in cloud computing all demonstrated the power of innovation in transforming industries. Meanwhile, Yahoo! failed to develop new, groundbreaking products. Its acquisitions—such as Flickr and Tumblr—were promising, but Yahoo! struggled to integrate them into its core business and leverage their full potential.

Yahoo!'s story serves as a cautionary tale about the dangers of complacency. In the tech world, innovation is not a one-time event but a continuous process. Companies that rest on their laurels, relying on past successes, can quickly be overtaken by competitors that are more agile and forward-thinking. Yahoo!'s inability to foster a culture of ongoing innovation was a major factor in its decline.

4. User Experience Is King

Another key lesson from Yahoo!'s story is the importance of user experience. While Yahoo! initially thrived by offering a broad array of services—such as email, news, and entertainment—it eventually became bogged down by its sprawling product offerings. Users were overwhelmed by Yahoo!'s cluttered homepage, which attempted to be a one-stop shop for everything but lacked focus.

In contrast, Google's minimalist search page and Facebook's streamlined social media platform offered users a much simpler and more focused experience. This allowed them to dominate their respective fields by focusing on doing one thing exceptionally well—search for Google and social networking for Facebook. Yahoo!, by trying to do everything, ended up diluting its brand and confusing users.

The lesson here is that a company's success depends heavily on providing a clear and compelling user experience. Tech companies must prioritize simplicity, usability, and focus in their products. Yahoo!'s attempt to cater to everyone resulted in a disjointed user experience, making it difficult for the company to retain loyal users in the face of more specialized competitors.

5. Adapting to Changing Market Trends

In the rapidly evolving tech world, companies must be able to adapt to changing market trends. Yahoo!'s downfall can be partially attributed to its failure to recognize and adapt to two major trends: the rise of mobile technology and the shift toward cloud computing.

As smartphones became the primary way people accessed the internet, Yahoo! lagged behind in developing mobile-friendly services. Competitors like Google and Facebook quickly optimized their platforms for mobile, while Yahoo! was slow to respond. By the time Yahoo! began focusing on mobile technology under Marissa Mayer's leadership, it was already too late to regain significant market share.

Similarly, Yahoo! was slow to embrace cloud computing, an area where Amazon and Google made significant strides. Yahoo!'s reluctance to invest heavily in cloud infrastructure and services meant that it missed out on a major growth area in the tech industry.

The key takeaway is that tech companies must remain agile and responsive to emerging trends. Those that fail to adapt to shifts in technology, user behavior, and market demands risk falling behind their more innovative competitors.

6. Leadership and Strategic Vision Matter

Finally, Yahoo!'s story underscores the importance of strong leadership and a clear strategic vision. Over the years, Yahoo! experienced significant turnover in its executive leadership, with multiple CEOs cycling through the company. This lack of stability made it difficult for Yahoo! to execute a cohesive long-term strategy.

Under Marissa Mayer, Yahoo! attempted to refocus its efforts on mobile technology and content, but despite her high-profile hiring and aggressive acquisition strategy, the company continued to struggle. Mayer's leadership was marked by ambitious plans, such as the acquisition of Tumblr, but without a clear vision of how these moves fit into a larger strategy, Yahoo! could not regain its former dominance.

Leadership in tech companies must not only have a vision but also the ability to execute it effectively. Yahoo!'s rotating leadership and inconsistent strategic direction hindered its ability to stay competitive in the rapidly changing internet landscape.

Conclusion: Learning from Yahoo!'s Journey

Yahoo!'s rise and fall offer valuable lessons for tech companies navigating the complexities of the digital age. Its early success was driven by innovation, timing, and foresight, but its decline was marked by missed opportunities, strategic missteps, and a failure to adapt to the changing landscape. From its inability to acquire Google and Facebook to its struggle with innovation and user experience, Yahoo!'s story serves as a cautionary tale for internet giants looking to stay relevant.

The technology industry is unforgiving, and companies that fail to innovate, adapt, and maintain a strong strategic vision can quickly be overtaken by more agile competitors. Yahoo!'s journey highlights the need for continuous innovation, a focus on user experience, and leadership with the foresight to anticipate and respond to market trends. These lessons are critical for any tech company looking to thrive in the fast-paced world of the internet.

Conclusion: Yahoo!'s Enduring Legacy

Yahoo! may no longer be the dominant internet force it once was, but its contributions to the early web are undeniable. It was one of the original architects of the internet era, pioneering innovations in email, search engines, and digital news that helped shape how billions of people interact with the web today. The rise, fall, and reinvention of Yahoo! serve as a powerful narrative about the potential and pitfalls of the tech world—an industry defined by rapid evolution, fierce competition, and the constant pressure to innovate.

Yahoo!'s Role in Shaping the Early Web
In the mid-1990s, as the internet began to grow beyond academic and military institutions, Yahoo! became one of the first companies to make the web accessible to the average user. Before Yahoo!, navigating the internet was a daunting task for most people. Websites were largely unorganized, and the tools to search for information were either rudimentary or non-existent. Yahoo! changed that. It was one of the first platforms to organize the web in a user-friendly way, creating a searchable directory that helped people discover the information they needed.

Yahoo!'s early innovations were fundamental to the development of the internet as a mainstream tool. Its search engine, Yahoo! Mail, and content offerings like Yahoo! News and Yahoo! Finance provided a one-stop portal for users, turning Yahoo! into an essential part of the daily online experience. At its peak, Yahoo! was not just a web directory but a hub for all internet activities. It laid the groundwork for what we now consider standard online services.

Lessons from Yahoo!'s Decline

As much as Yahoo!'s rise was remarkable, its fall from dominance provides valuable lessons for both businesses and individuals navigating the fast-paced tech world. One of the key lessons from Yahoo!'s decline is the importance of innovation and focus. Despite its early success, Yahoo! was slow to adapt to the shifting dynamics of the internet. The company struggled to develop its own search technology to compete with Google, which quickly became the leader in search by focusing on delivering more accurate and relevant results.

Yahoo!'s decision to expand in too many directions without mastering any one area—such as its ventures into social media, advertising, and content production—left it spread thin and unable to compete with more focused and agile competitors like Facebook and Google. The lesson here is clear: in the ever-evolving tech industry, companies must remain laser-focused on their core strengths while staying agile enough to embrace new technologies and business models.

Yahoo! also serves as a case study in the importance of strategic vision. Over the years, Yahoo! missed key opportunities to acquire industry-changing companies like Google and Facebook, decisions that ultimately contributed to its downfall. These missed acquisitions highlight the importance of long-term thinking and the ability to recognize disruptive technologies before they fully take root.

Yahoo!'s Reinvention and Lasting Impact

While Yahoo! has faced significant challenges, it has not disappeared. Under new ownership by Verizon, Yahoo! has been refocusing on its core offerings, particularly Yahoo! Finance, Yahoo! Mail, and Yahoo! Sports. These services, while perhaps not as dominant as they once were, continue to attract millions of loyal users. Yahoo! Finance, in particular, has emerged as one of the most trusted sources for financial news and tools, catering to both casual users and professional investors. This reinvention of Yahoo! around its core strengths is a testament to the company's enduring relevance in the digital age.

Another lasting impact of Yahoo! is its influence on the digital advertising landscape. While it may not have outpaced Google in the search advertising space, Yahoo! was a pioneer in early online advertising models, from banner ads to display networks. The company's advertising strategies and infrastructure helped lay the foundation for what would become a multibillion-dollar industry, and its legacy can still be felt in today's programmatic and targeted ad technologies.

Yahoo!'s foray into digital content also had a profound influence on how media is consumed on the internet. Yahoo! News and Yahoo! Sports were some of the first mainstream online news platforms, and they showed that the internet could be a legitimate space for real-time information. They paved the way for countless other digital news outlets, many of which owe their origins to Yahoo!'s groundbreaking content strategies.

The Future of Yahoo!
Looking ahead, Yahoo!'s future will depend on its ability to continue innovating and adapting to the ever-changing digital landscape. The internet of today is vastly different from the one that Yahoo! dominated in the late 1990s. The rise of artificial intelligence, the growth of social media, and the increasing importance of mobile technology have all reshaped how users interact with the web. Yahoo!'s challenge will be to stay relevant by aligning itself with these new trends while building on its trusted services.

There are opportunities for Yahoo! to make a comeback in niche areas, especially as internet users become more selective in how they consume content and access services. Yahoo! Finance and Yahoo! Sports, for example, continue to have strong user bases, and the company's deep data sets could give it a competitive edge in areas like personalized content and financial tools. With the right investments in AI, machine learning, and data analytics, Yahoo! could once again position itself as a leader in these specific fields.

Furthermore, as concerns over data privacy and cybersecurity grow, Yahoo! could capitalize on its long-standing relationship with users by emphasizing security and trust. Yahoo! Mail, despite competition from Google and Microsoft, still serves millions of users, many of whom have been with the service for decades. Focusing on enhancing security features and offering premium services could be a way for Yahoo! to stand out in a crowded market.

Yahoo! as a Symbol of the Internet's Evolution

Perhaps the most enduring legacy of Yahoo! is that it symbolizes the early internet era. For millions of users, Yahoo! was their first experience with the internet—a portal that connected them to the world's information. It represents the promise of the internet as a place of discovery, connection, and opportunity.

The rise and fall of Yahoo! mirrors the evolution of the internet itself. From the days of simple web directories and basic email services to the complex ecosystems of search, social media, and AI-driven content, Yahoo!'s journey reflects the challenges and triumphs that come with rapid technological change. The company's story is not just about one business, but about the entire arc of the internet age—from the wild experimentation of the 1990s to the consolidation and innovation of the 2000s and beyond.

Conclusion: Yahoo!'s Place in Internet History

Yahoo!'s story is far from over. While it may no longer be the titan of the internet that it once was, its role in shaping the early web and its lasting contributions to digital content, advertising, and email are secure in the annals of internet history. Yahoo! will be remembered as one of the internet's pioneers, a company that helped bring the web into millions of homes and changed the way we interact with information.

As the digital age continues to evolve, so too will Yahoo!'s place within it. Whether through reinvention, adaptation, or collaboration, Yahoo!'s journey will continue to offer lessons for businesses and individuals navigating the dynamic world of technology. While its dominance may have waned, Yahoo!'s enduring legacy is a reminder of the transformative power of the internet—and of the importance of staying ahead of the curve in an ever-changing world.

Bibliography

1. **The Search: How Google and Its Rivals Rewrote the Rules of Business and Transformed Our Culture** by John Battelle

A detailed exploration of how Google transformed the internet, providing context on search engines, including Yahoo!'s role.

2. **Marissa Mayer and the Fight to Save Yahoo!** by Nicholas Carlson

Focused on Marissa Mayer's leadership at Yahoo!, this book offers insights into the company's strategies during her tenure.

3. **The Yahoo! Story: Yahoo!'s Rise to Internet Greatness and Its Fall** by Jeffrey F. Rayport

A focused narrative on Yahoo!'s early days, growth, and the strategic missteps that led to its decline.

4. **Googled: The End of the World as We Know It** by Ken Auletta

This book delves into Google's impact on the digital world, offering useful contrasts with Yahoo!'s trajectory.

5. **In the Plex: How Google Thinks, Works, and Shapes Our Lives** by Steven Levy

A comprehensive look at Google's evolution, which contrasts with Yahoo!'s struggles and missed opportunities.

6. **Chaos Monkeys: Obscene Fortune and Random Failure in Silicon Valley** by Antonio García Martínez

Offers a behind-the-scenes look at Silicon Valley, where Yahoo! competed, made deals, and missed out on key acquisitions.

7. **The Innovators: How a Group of Hackers, Geniuses, and Geeks Created the Digital Revolution** by Walter Isaacson

Covers the key players in the digital revolution, including Yahoo!, showing its significance in internet history.

8. **Disrupted: My Misadventure in the Start-Up Bubble** by Dan Lyons

A humorous look into the chaotic world of Silicon Valley, where Yahoo! was a key player, providing context for the company's decline amidst the tech boom.

Acknowledgments

Writing *Yahoo! Through the Ages: The Rise, Fall, and Reinvention of an Internet Giant* has been an incredible journey, and I am deeply grateful to all the individuals and organizations that made this book possible.

First and foremost, I would like to express my heartfelt thanks to the founders of Yahoo!, Jerry Yang and David Filo, whose pioneering work shaped the internet as we know it today. Their vision inspired me to dive deep into the history of this iconic company.

A special thank you goes to the former and current employees of Yahoo! whose contributions, both in successes and challenges, helped form the complex and fascinating story of this internet giant. I am grateful to those who shared their insights, stories, and experiences, providing invaluable context to the rise and transformation of Yahoo!.

I would also like to extend my gratitude to the researchers, journalists, and historians who documented Yahoo!'s journey over the years. Their work provided the foundation for many of the key moments explored in this book, and their commitment to capturing the details of Yahoo!'s evolution made my task much easier.

To the tech industry analysts and experts who helped me understand the intricate technical, business, and strategic decisions behind Yahoo!'s milestones, thank you. Your knowledge enriched this project and allowed me to tell a more informed and nuanced story.

I am also deeply appreciative of my editor, whose guidance and feedback helped shape this book into what it is today. Your keen eye and relentless pursuit of clarity have been invaluable.

To my family and friends, thank you for your patience, encouragement, and unwavering support. Writing a book requires immense time and focus, and your belief in me kept me motivated every step of the way.

Finally, to the readers, thank you for your curiosity and interest in the story of Yahoo!. I hope this book sheds light on the dynamic and ever-changing world of technology and the companies that shape it. It is through your engagement that stories like Yahoo!'s continue to live on and inspire future generations.

With sincere gratitude,
Zahid Ameer
Versatile Indie Author

Disclaimer

The information provided in this book, *Yahoo! Through the Ages: The Rise, Fall, and Reinvention of an Internet Giant*, is intended for informational and educational purposes only. While every effort has been made to ensure the accuracy of the information contained herein, the author and publisher make no representations or warranties with respect to the completeness, accuracy, or timeliness of the contents of this book.

This book is not endorsed by, affiliated with, or sponsored by Yahoo! Inc., Verizon Media, or any other associated entities. All product names, trademarks, and registered trademarks are the property of their respective owners. The inclusion of any names or brands within this book is for informational purposes and does not imply endorsement or partnership.

The opinions and interpretations expressed are those of the author and are based on publicly available information and research. Readers are encouraged to conduct their own independent research and consult with professionals for advice on specific topics.

The author and publisher shall not be held liable for any damages or loss arising from the use or interpretation of the information in this book.

Yahoo! Through the Ages

About me

I am Zahid Ameer, hailing from the vibrant country of India. As an author, ghostwriter, bibliophile, online affiliate marketer, blogger, YouTuber, graphic designer, and animal lover, I have woven my passions into a unique tapestry that defines my life's work.

Born and raised in India, I have always possessed a deep love for literature. With an insatiable appetite for books, I have amassed an impressive collection of around 1,600 titles, predominantly in English. My passion for reading brings me immense joy and serves as a source of inspiration for my writing endeavors.

I have compiled an impressive portfolio of written works as an author and ghostwriter. With a captivating writing style and an innate ability to craft engaging narratives, I bring my stories to life, captivating readers from all walks of life. My wide range of interests and experiences contribute to the richness of my writing, allowing me to connect with my audience on a heartfelt level effortlessly.

Beyond my literary pursuits, I have also established a strong presence on various digital platforms. I utilize my YouTube channel and blog to raise awareness about all types of knowledge and to share heartwarming stories of animals. Using my platform to shed light on important issues, I strive to create a world where humans and animals can coexist harmoniously.

In addition to my work as an author, I have also dabbled in the world of affiliate marketing. With my webpreneur spirit, I have ventured into online marketing, leveraging my knowledge and skills to promote products and services that align with my values.

However, my most cherished role is that of a father. Family is at the core of my being, and everything I do is centered around creating a better future for my loved ones. My dedication to my family is evident in my passion for personal growth and my relentless pursuit of success. Through my various endeavors, I strive to set an example of perseverance and ambition for my children, inspiring them to chase their dreams unapologetically.

In a world where specialization often dominates, I defy convention by embracing multiple passions and excelling in diverse fields. My love for books, animals, and family has become the driving force behind my achievements. By the grace of Almighty God, my unique blend of characteristics has allowed me to leave an indelible mark on the world, enriching the lives of those I encounter along the way.

To your grand success in life,

Zahid Ameer
Versatile Indie Author

www.ingramcontent.com/pod-product-compliance
Lightning Source LLC
LaVergne TN
LVHW022126060326
832903LV00063B/4258